The Dowager Empress

The publisher gratefully acknowledges the support of the Canada Council for the Arts and the Ontario Arts Council. The publisher is also grateful for the financial assistance received from the Government of Canada.

Front cover artwork: Tamara Stone, "Stone Ship's Journey," 2019, mixed media, 3.6 x 5 inches.

Front cover design: Val Fullard

Library and Archives Canada Cataloguing in Publication

Title: The dowager empress : selected poems of Adele Wiseman /
edited by Elizabeth Greene. Other titles: Poems. Selections
Names: Wiseman, Adele, author. | Greene, Elizabeth, 1943– editor.
Series: Inanna poetry & fiction series.
Description: Series statement: Inanna poetry & fiction series
Identifiers: Canadiana (print) 2019014789X | Canadiana (ebook) 20190147903 |
ISBN 9781771336895 (softcover) | ISBN 9781771336901 (epub) | ISBN 9781771336918
(Kindle) | ISBN 9781771336925 (pdf)
Classification: LCC PS8545.I85 A6 2019 | DDC C811/.54—dc23

Printed and bound in Canada

MIX
Paper from
responsible sources
FSC® C004071

Inanna Publications and Education Inc.
210 Founders College, York University
4700 Keele Street, Toronto, Ontario M3J 1P3 Canada
Telephone: (416) 736–5356   Fax (416) 736–5765
Email: inanna.publications@inanna.ca Website: www.inanna.ca

The Dowager Empress

POEMS BY
ADELE WISEMAN

— *edited by* —
Elizabeth Greene

inanna poetry & fiction series

INANNA Publications and Education Inc.
Toronto, Canada

Contents

Mysteries of Flight

Spaces

The Dowager Empress Suite

Introduction

Adele Wiseman's poetry, mostly unpublished before now, is the work of her last ten years. From 1981 to 1986 she wrote hundreds of poems, enough for six or seven short collections. She saved three hundred and thirty-two in a final box of poetry (Adele Wiseman Fonds, F0447, Clara Thomas Archives, Scott Library, York University), but others that she discarded in the final selection, worked on and revised, show her process and are often fine. Some of them are included here.

As a writer, Adele was always trying something new. One of her poems says it best:

> I CANNOT BREAK FAITH
> LET OTHERS DO
> WHAT THEY CAN DO
> LET ME DO WHAT
> ONLY I CAN DO
> ("I CANNOT," November 4, 1984)

She wrote what she felt she had to, took risks, tried the unexpected. So, after her 1956 Governor-General's award-winning novel, *The Sacrifice*, she wrote a long, unpublished and unperformed play *The Lovebound*, about a ship full of Jewish refugees, the St. Louis, which was refused at port after port and finally returned to Nazi Germany. Her play is particularly timely in 2019 when unprecedented numbers of refugees are fleeing; many are in limbo; and some are being returned over borders back into danger. *The Lovebound* was followed by Adele's second novel *Crackpot,* rejected many times before Margaret Atwood's prescient criticism allowed Adele to revise it to reach its present form, and Margaret Laurence steered it to McClelland & Stewart (see Panofsky

83-84). Jack McClelland disliked the title, but didn't insist that Adele change it—and the title does lead into the theme of broken pots, cracked vessels, and the scattered pieces, the Tikkun Olam myth that Adele invokes in her epigraph. *Crackpot* was published in 1974. Adele's next major work, *Old Woman at Play* (1978) is a memoir of her mother, a consideration of the dolls her mother made, a meditation on creativity through the dolls. The same fall, she had her play *Testimonial Dinner* printed privately. Her essays, *Memoirs of a Book Molesting Childhood,* were published by Oxford in 1987.

Some constants underlie Adele's varied writing career: the Jewish immigrant experience, commitment to the margins (Hoda, the heroine of *Crackpot*, is overweight and supports herself and her father by prostitution—"doing the worst thing for the best reason," said Adele (qtd. in Meyer and O'Riordan).

Danile, Hoda's father, is blind; Adele's mother in *Old Woman at Play* is dying of cancer; the three children in Adele's final, brilliant story, "Goon of the Moon and the Expendables" are in a home for challenged children: Josh, the main character, has trouble walking and speaking; Lucinda who "has the freshest laugh" is in a wheelchair and perhaps has a bad heart; Gordon, the Goon of the title, has a stent in his head. Adele's choice of character and subject matter clashes with current celebrity bright and shiny culture of easy answers.

In 1981, having written novels, plays, a memoir and essays, she began writing poetry. "What started Adele writing poetry so suddenly?" I asked Arlene Lampert, Adele's close friend when I interviewed her for *We Who Can Fly* in 1996 (Greene).

"I don't know what started her writing poetry," Arlene said. "During that time I was living in Spain and California for about four years in a row. I know around '83 or '84 I was up visiting, and there was this huge manuscript of poems. I don't know why everything she wanted to say suddenly started to pop out in poems, and she didn't have an explanation for it" (Greene 57). Arlene added that at this time, Adele was spending a lot of time with poets and going to poetry readings endlessly (Greene 57).

My own guess was that Adele had fallen in love with a poet. He had blue eyes (her first poem tells us). I have not saved my reading notes from the fall of 1995, but I wrote in *We Who Can Fly*: "The poetry begins with a series of love poems" (Greene 97).

This short series is no longer in the archive. The first poem, "Eyes meet, you smile" still begins the first folder of the first box, but the only other poem I remember of this series (maybe six poems) shows the poet walking home up Avenue Road and the Loved One passing her in his car. Adele didn't save the "Eyes meet, you smile" poem among the three hundred and thirty-two of the last folder, nor did she save the other few poems of the sequence. She did, though, collect twenty-two of the shorter love poems in a folder, "In Our Play," and it's clear that the Loved One by this time seems based on more than one person or has possibly become entirely fictional—in one poem he has green eyes; in another, slitty eyes. My guess, unverified, is that the poems began with unrequited love, and though the unrequited love was a constant theme, the Loved One's identity morphed.

In any case, Adele did not write for commercial success. She did do "what only she could do," made hard choices, always setting herself new challenges. She didn't repeat. The price of these hard choices was her difficulty publishing truly original works. She never wrote anything as successful as *The Sacrifice*. But each of her subsequent books is an achievement, authentic and vision-clearing. Each book has its own delights, as does the poetry.

Adele Wiseman is often regarded as a novelist who, tragically, only wrote two novels. It would be more accurate to call her a writer who tried many forms. The peaks of her achievement (in my view) are *The Sacrifice; The Lovebound; Crackpot; Old Woman at Play; Memoirs of a Book Molesting Childhood*; her poetry 1981-86; "The Dowager Empress Suite" (the long poem written from 1987 or so until her death in 1992); and the story "Goon of the Moon and the Expendables," published just before her death in the *Malahat Review*. There may be differing opinions about the height of each peak, but this is the range of Adele's literary accomplishment, solid, original, enduring, and largely unpublished or out of print.

I wish I could say that Adele Wiseman needs no introduction. But when I tell people I am editing her poetry, I get a lot of blank looks. I continue: "Margaret Laurence's best friend, her lifelong writing friend." I sometimes add, "She is the original of Ella in [Margaret Laurence's novel] *The Diviners*." Interestingly, Ella is a poet, even though *The Diviners* was written and published years before Adele started writing poetry. Sometimes art predicts life. But Ella is a minor character, and most people don't remember her (Lennox and Panofsky 319).

Anyone who reads the *Selected Letters of Margaret Laurence and Adele Wiseman*, edited by John Lennox and Ruth Panofsky, will see how close they were. They shared life news, of course, but the drama of the letters is in their shared writing news, the writing begun, in progress, finished, published or (in Adele's case) rejected. Margaret Laurence cabled Adele after Viking rejected *Crackpot* in 1968: VIKING IS IN SPAIN. TRAKNOPF. LETTER FOLLOWS. LOVE, MARGARET (*Viking is insane. Try Knopf*). Both friends got a great laugh over the mangled cable. In the letter that followed, Margaret Laurence wrote:

> …I don't believe and never have believed that you were writing for any one generation, Adele. That is what has made it so much more difficult for you than for me, and why the quick rewards which I have had (and let's face it, have mightily enjoyed) have not been open in the same way to you…. I felt very strongly about it then, [seventeen years before] that you might have hellish difficulty with everything you wrote, but had to keep on regardless, because your writing is the kind

that people do react strongly towards, either pro or con, and you mustn't be too conned by the cons, kid, because what you do is too valuable in the long run. Same thing happened with *The Lovebound,* and it will one day be published, as itself, as a play, or as I always tend to think of it, as a novel in play form, but published it will be. What angers me terribly is that it should have been published already. Adele, the same goddam thing is true of your new novel. The patterns haven't changed....

SOME WRITING IS DATELESS AND UNDATEABLE. IT DOESN'T SPEAK TO ANY ONE AGE ABOUT ITSELF. IT SPEAKS TO MAN ABOUT HIMSELF. (Lennox and Panofsky 262)

Only a truly close friend, deep in writing herself, could have written such a consoling letter with such deep understanding of Adele's process and of the writing process.

Adele Wiseman was gifted in friendship. She mentored many writers; she served as the Director of the May Studios at the Banff Studios from 1987 until her death, although ill health meant that she was only physically present at the May Studios for three of those years. When I was at Banff, in 1992, I felt the program's best gift was permission to aspire, not just to success, but to something more lasting. I think that was Adele's influence, even from afar.

I hope Adele's poetry will introduce her to you better than I could. Read the poems, and you will have a sense of who she was and is.

"I write myself here," Adele wrote on an idea note in 1984. As always, Adele is the best commentator on her own work. The early poems from 1981-1986 are very much in her own voice, not subsumed to characters, as in her fiction and plays. Even her essays and memoir of her mother are slightly more formal. It's not exactly the stuff of National Enquirer headlines, but the poems are the only place in Adele

Wiseman's writing where we see her dailiness: the poet looking out the window at grass and sunsets and worms, reacting to newspaper articles, the poet in love. It's not surprising that she writes about her daughter Tamara and her mother. By turns the speaker is wise, curious, tough, funny, longing, perceptive. The poet's intense life of the mind is rooted in ordinary moments. Where a novel is a world in itself, a poem catches a glance, a thought, a phrase and makes it something worth considering and saving. What makes the poetry worth reading for those who didn't know Adele Wiseman or her work is its depth, its authenticity, its easy handling of form, its readiness to break into a smile unexpectedly (as Adele Wiseman's prose sentences do as well). Adele's poetry is an excellent companion, vision-clearing, as all her work is.

Adele left three hundred thirty-two poems in her final folder and many others in the three earlier boxes. She had also collected two files of short verse: "In Our Play" (the love poems) and "Mysteries of Flight" (mostly nature poems). Each file contained twenty-two poems, but they are all short verse, and not all the short poems carry their weight in a collection like this one. I have kept her titles as section titles, but have added some poems and subtracted others. (A complete list of Adele's titles in these two files appears in the appendix). I have added two sections, the opening "Instructions from Poems in Progress" (poems about poetry) and "Spaces" (other poems I thought should be in this book that didn't belong anywhere else). The fifth section is Adele's last, ambitious, though not quite finished work, "The Dowager Empress Suite."

In ordering the poems, I have tried to let them speak to me and to one another, as I would in one of my own books or in the anthologies I have edited. I am aware that Adele might not have ordered the poems this way, or even chosen these particular poems. But if poems in progress have ideas of their own, so do collections. Adele is no longer available for consultation. I have had to ask the poems.

Instructions from Poems in Progress

The creative process is one of Adele Wiseman's great themes—and she doesn't privilege any one sort. In *Crackpot,* blind Danile is an artist figure as a teller of stories (compare Christie in *The Diviners*) and a maker of exquisite, almost too-perfect baskets. His daughter, Hoda, calls herself an artist of love, someone who "makes love." Also she has the artist's gift of (occasionally) jumping inside other peoples' minds. In *Old Woman at Play,* Adele's central focus is on her mother, Chaika Waisman, maker of dolls—and she shows us Chaika's process of creating a doll from bits that inspire her: a piece of fishbone, buttons, leftover cloth, old stockings, Adele's Governor-General's medal. These discarded bits build into characters and lives (Chaika always makes the dolls in pairs) with their own stories. Chaika's doll-making, Adele's writing, Tamara's art—Adele doesn't judge between different forms of creativity. Here, in the poetry, though, she focuses on poetry, on her own voice, her own process and advice (to herself or to any of us who want to listen):

> Never put a poem off
> It's a vain capricious thing
> You may put off eating
> You may defer play
> You may even, briefly,
> Put your love away
> But ask a flash of verse to wait
> Till you find pencil, pen or slate
> In vain,
> You'll never see that joy
> Made word again.

Adele took her own advice. The files are interleaved with idea notes, sometimes with ideas written on paper napkins, or, once, on a Boots pharmacy shopping bag.

But ideas are only the beginning. Adele explores and details her poetic process in her remarkable long poem, almost a road map, "Instructions from Poems in Progress" which begins with the poem saying "Find me" and insists (a section later) that "The poem tells itself" and continues:

> It begins in
> revelation's crucible
> passionate mind.
> Idea of a poem
> waits on voice;
> voice waits on
> idea of a poem.

This short poem goes dancing off into typeset, but the longer poem, the "Instructions" is barely begun. One of the joys of the poem are the perfect aphorisms embedded in it:

> To discover what you want to say
> you have to try to say it.

and

> Welcome surprises.
> Ignore temptation of
> the easy and familiar
> They will quickly bore.

These could serve as epigraphs to a critical book on Adele's work.

The instructions are mingled with imagery—where does the poem come from? Esker and drumlin, midden heaps, scraps (think of Chaika

Waisman's dolls), but also art, master work. The instructions continue:

> You should always be surprised by the end result.
> It's the moment when you learn what you've been about.
> +
> Do not resent time spent.
> The final poem
> no matter how strenuously won
> is always given.

I have selected a few quotations here, but the whole poem could serve as a mini-poetry workshop, a reminder that each poem is its own journey, and the result of the completion of the process is another poem saying "Find me."

In Our Play

Unrequited love is not one of the master narratives of our age, but it is a master narrative. Adele's love poetry clearly formed a compelling body of work when I first read the poems in the fall of 1995, even though the poems were not all together. The poems began with "Eyes meet, you smile" with its great image of drowning deep in the blue of the Loved One's eyes. As I have said, the identity of the Loved One morphs, and may be, in the end, totally fictional; but the poet's longing is consistent, as is the Loved One's standoffishness.

When I interviewed Arlene Lampert in 1996, I asked her if she had any idea who the Loved One might be. She answered that she was sure he was fictional, but if he weren't (she laughed), she would be sure to ask Adele who he was the minute they met on the Other Side.

Adele collected twenty-two of the love poems in the folder, "In Our Play." But she limited herself in this collection by sticking to short verse. Some of the longer poems give the arc of the story more substance, and

I have edited the contents of the folder, excising some short poems, including some longer ones. Adele arranged her poems along a story line, and I have tried to honour that, beginning with "Eyes meet you smile" and ending with the formal, generous sonnet "Send Not Regrets" which concludes:

> Though you deny us harmony of hearts
> I'll bless you in the singing of my parts.

and with the wistful

> It's winter now.
> What shall I do with all this love gone stale?

The title poem "In Our Play" suggests literary fiction (a play, dramatic form), "just" playing around, and sex (contrary to fact):

> In our play
> performance of the parts
> is always touching....

> In the climax of our play
> the parts come
> together

There is a lovely wistfulness in this poem, but also a smile as the poet moves between the different meanings of the word. The poet's feelings and longing are genuine, but only in "our play," constructed by the poet, do the parts come together.

There must have been telephone calls:

> The silent telephone

always about to burst
into true love.

There must also have been times

the Loved One didn't call:
Loved one,
You said you would call
again.
Should I hold my breath
again?

Adele does "write herself" in these sometimes yearning, sometimes resigned love poems. But no matter where these poems started, no matter what the relationship of art to life, the arc of the story is a construct, emphasized by the title Adele chose for the folder of short verse, created by a skilled novelist. Although I have included some longer poems and omitted others, I have tried to follow the shape of the story as Adele presented it, with the title poem somewhere in the middle of the sequence.

Mysteries of Flight

Adele's daughter, Tamara Stone, told me that she and Adele were both fascinated by the Daedalus/Icarus myth. For Adele, ability to fly was one the marks of the artist. "Mysteries of Flight" is the title of the other folder of short verse Adele selected. It includes winged poems—birds, bats, bees, falling leaves—but also nature poems, including haiku and sunset poems. Again, I have included longer poems, trying to use flight as the central theme with nature as a secondary theme. Where do poems come from? Some from myth; some from thought or daydream; some from looking out the window.

I have begun this section with the lovely poem, "Currents," for Tamara, Adele's partner in flight:

> Those of us who fly
> know currents,
> learn tricks from birds,
> the skill to navigate
> the invisible
> take off into the wind.

The exhilaration of flight: the artist's freedom to soar and "navigate/ the invisibleBut this is counterpoised by "Ascent."

> Ascent is sheet delight,
> but sudden birds must face
> a danger of return
> so swift it baffles flight....

> The perilous moment
> for all high flyers
> is the descent.

In spite of the caution, this section sparkles with the joy of flight—starlings, gulls, bats in flight, little birds "peeping holes in the dark/to let in the dawn." This section also shows Adele's delight in nature—something she doesn't allow herself in her other work.

The eight well-turned haiku Adele included in this folder are typical of her command of this form, at the other end of the scale from her lengthy novel *Crackpot* and her long play *The Lovebound*. She also included four summer sunset poems, variations on a theme, ending with the joking lines in "Standards": "Let's face it/ Nature has no class." I have kept all four in this selection to show how Adele worked and reworked ideas, especially evident in the progress of her poems from idea notes or jottings to finished works throughout the first three works-in-progress boxes in her fonds.

The first part of Adele's folder is mostly summer; the second part is mostly autumn. I have concluded this part with a longer poem, "Autumn Days":

> Autumn days
> the messy time of year
> the time I'm most at home in

Falling leaves are part of flight (Adele has more than one poem on them), even if they are descending only. The last two lines are arresting. Arlene Lampert said of Adele "…the chaos she was comfortable living in would have driven me mad…. Her house was strewn with papers and bits…" (Greene 58). This suggests that Adele's very formed work was done, at least during the years of her friendship with Arlene Lampert, with papers and bits about her, perhaps something like leaves?

Although much of Adele's poetry shows a responsiveness to the seasons, "Mysteries of Flight" is the most rooted in weather, the seasons, close observation of nature. "Autumn Days" exemplifies all of this.

Spaces

> It's not the words the danger's in, it's in
> the drops between, it's in the spaces of the dream
> we fall….

"Spaces" was one of the few poems published in Adele's lifetime. It appeared in Rosemary Sullivan's *Poetry by Canadian Women*, along with "Ascent" and "Roofers."

I have included in this section poems too powerful to be left out of this introduction to Adele's poetry. These are the darkest poems in this book, interwoven with falling, death, a dark political vision. They range from the humorous "The Gifted Itch Scratcher"—anyone who is one or knows one will recognize the truth of it—to political poems like "That Nascent Evil":

> That nascent evil against which
> you will not raise your voice today,
> tomorrow, fully grown,
> will not allow you to raise your head.

The few political poems in this section stand in for many others. Readers of other works by Adele know how very political she was. I have also included two elegiac poems for Adele's mother Chaika Waisman (readers of the essay "Lucky Mom" or *Old Woman at Play* will recognize the material) and two poems on night, one for children, "What Is the Night: a fancy for children," and the terrifying but unforgettable, "The Void" which begins:

> The Void before, Death stalking me behind,
> yet I must move, and where I enter
> Emptiness escapes, flees me,
> as I flee my pursuer

This is Adele's version of Chopin's *Dead March*, a tour de force. It is dated June, 1984. (The light-hearted children's fancy is dated July, 1985). All Adele's writing took courage and unswerving vision—that is especially evident in "The Void."

The Dowager Empress

"Have you read "The Dowager Empress?" I asked Arlene Lampert when I interviewed her in the fall of 1996. Mary Cameron and Steven Heighton remembered Adele reading from it at Banff in 1991, and I was starting to see it hanging in the air beyond my reach and reading. (It wasn't in the archives in 1995—it probably arrived in 1996).

"Oh yes," Arlene answered. "Isn't it in the York University Archives? It probably is now.... Such a complex piece of writing—and so political and so ambitious—so intricate." Arlene added, "She had a lot she wanted to say about politics, about woman, about moral issues, and she had a lot of it in that poem." (Greene 58)

I had wanted to read "The Dowager Empress" (correct title "The Dowager Empress Suite") for twenty years. But when I returned to York, to the archive now named for the great scholar and critic Clara Thomas, I needed help from an archivist to find the file folder squeezed against the back of the last box of poetry in the Adele Wiseman Fonds. Moments of arrival can be so simple—there was the long-awaited sequence of poems spread out before me.

I knew from the title that the poem (or suite) would go against the grain—dowagers are usually minor characters, not Empresses—and that it would be a feminist revisionist view of rulership. But when the actual lines on the actual pages were finally before me, I was thrown off balance, and I had to read the suite several times before it came into focus. In a way I wasn't surprised. Adele tended not to do what her readers expected.

"The Dowager Empress Suite" is part folk-tale, part fable, part transformation myth. It is a sequence of events beginning with the death of the Emperor, concluding ten thousand years later with the legacy of the Empress. The writing is highly formal with a great deal of rhyme, word play and internal rhyme. The tight form and formal language underline the poem's, and Adele's, essentially comic vision. Comedy can contain tragedy, as Dante's *Divine Comedy* does, and Chaucer's *Troilus and Criseyde*, and Shakespeare's *The Tempest* and *The Winter's Tale*. In high comedy the comic and the serious are fused, but the writing may break into smiles unexpectedly, and the underlying vision is orderly, not chaotic.

The poem needs to be read on three levels at once: the intricate, formal, delightful surface; the dramatic incidents of the narrative; the "things Adele had to say about politics, about women, about moral issues" tied to the incidents but resonating beneath them. The carefully wrought language helps legitimize the radical feminist politics underneath—the political structure plays against the gorgeous surface.

According to Tamara, the suite is unfinished. It is hard to guess what is left undone. It is Adele's last major piece—she worked on it for several years—"until she couldn't," Tamara said.

The suite begins with the death of the Emperor at the end of his ten thousand year reign. His prized caged birds somehow escape and flutter comically beyond the reach of their eunuch keepers, enjoying their liberation and the game of flitting just beyond recapture. Birds, like angels, are winged ("Mysterious angels shed their dross"), the leap from bird to angel preparing us for a poem that includes transformation beyond realism, and the birds/angels remind us of the importance of birds/flight/wings in Adele's poetry before this poem.

Then the archers shoot the birds. The poem turns bloody. The eunuchs hide, fearing the Emperor's legendary anger—and the Emperor's anger at the birds' escape is so immense that "the Emperor's kettle whistles shrill/his blood is on the boil"—thwarted by his birds beyond his control, he expires.

The Empress grieves his death, but she also awakens as she comes into her own power (this is echoed later in the suite when her daughter, having raised *her* own children, awakens and seems ready to claim her power). The Empress' first speech is gracious. But she says, decisively, "Like my spouse ... I mean to rule alone."

Her first decrees are punishments—of the birds, leaving them free to fly and take their chances with the elements; of the eunuchs, giving them the birds' task of singing. She adds that there will be no more eunuchs made, and when the voices of the present troupe give out, women will sing—women who need no physical modification to find their voices. These decrees seem do not seem punitive; rather, just and liberating.

One hallmark of her rule is to gather all sorts of artists, musicians, poets, astrologers, philosophers around her. She is a patron of the arts. These few lines may remind us that Adele was the Director of the May Studios at Banff when she wrote "The Dowager Empress Suite," and, for the time she was at Banff, she lived in the centre of a creative ferment. Wouldn't we expect a woman ruler to foster the arts?

Power is not without its dangers. an unspecified amount of time passes before the next section, when the Dowager Empress, swathed in yellow and veiled, is preparing to ascend the Celestial Tower to renew the kingdom for the coming year. Shockingly, her guard follows her up the forbidden stair and attacks her with his sword, kills her and throws her from the tower. But, miraculously, or cleverly, the figure thrown from the tower is not the Empress—it is her favourite eunuch in disguise. At the end of the section the Dowager herself waits in the throne room for her son, the instigator of the attempted revolt, and peace returns.

As the Empress's ten-thousand-year reign progresses, her advisor suggests the need for a navy. She builds one ship—and sits on the deck overlooking the palace lawn.

When the advisor tells her the cost of the navy has caused her people financial hardship, she decrees when any of her people die, they will be given a splendid funeral in return for their service to the Navy. When the advisor protests the cost of these funerals, she replies, "Cheaper far than war."

The Empress's reign has brought prosperity to the kingdom. The arts have flourished. But toward the end of her ten thousand years, the eunuchs begin to plead for more eunuchs—they want heirs. They argue that poor boys might be delighted to trade their manhood for an easy life in the palace. Adele leaves us to draw our own conclusions about this. But in other ways, things seem to be slipping back to the "usual" after ten thousand years. Peace begins to pall. The second attempt on the Empress's life is successful—except no blood pours from her wounds, only feathers, which cause the assailants to flail and cough. In fine folk-tale fashion, the Empress has been transformed into a bird, not a flesh and blood bird, but all feathers (the reader might think of the transformation of the aging artist into a golden bird on a golden bough in "Sailing to Byzantium.") The transformation of the Empress is more comic—the assassination, though successful, turns into a pillow fight. But in the end, the rule of the Dowager Empress is over. But as Adele says in "Instructions from Poems in Progress": a poem should surprise. The ending of "The Dowager Empress Suite" is pure myth:

> Deep in the place where the Empire was
> a cult exists of birds
> who worship the Dowager Empress in feathers
> believe that when you sneeze her voice is blessing you
> and know she will always be there
> where you lay your egg at night
> and hatch your dreams.

The suite of poems which began as political ends in consolation and transmutation of the Empress as ruler to spiritual helper and guide.

"The Dowager Empress Suite" is essentially a comic poem. (It would probably make a great opera). It contains serious ideas about peace and war, about the alliance of feminism with peace, nurturing of the arts, good governance. It ends with a transcendent comic vision, of the Dowager Empress almost as Mother Goose, or angel, or goddess, as blesser of sneezes—a consolation to all of us with allergies—and dreams, a vision from beyond the veil, of the dead reaching back to the living.

As a writer, Adele is always ready to break into a smile, sometimes when you least expect it, though as a writer, she also provides the serious base necessary for successful, lasting comedy.

—Elizabeth Greene

References

Greene, Elizabeth, ed. *We Who Can Fly: Poems, Essays and Memories in Honour of Adele Wiseman.* Dunvegan, ON: Cormorant, 1997

Laurence, Margaret. *The Diviners.* Toronto: McClelland & Stewart, 1974.

Lennox, John and Ruth Panofsky, eds. *Selected Letters of Margaret Laurence and Adele Wiseman.* Toronto: University of Toronto Press, 1997.

Meyer, Bruce and Brian O'Riordan. "The Permissible and the Possible: An Interview With Adele Wiseman," *Lives & Works: Interviews.* Windsor, ON: Black Moss Press, 1992

Panofsky, Ruth. *The Force of Vocation: The Literary Career of Adele Wiseman,* Winnipeg: University of Manitoba Press, 2006.

Sullivan, Rosemary. *Poetry by Canadian Women.* Toronto: Oxford University Press, 1989.

Wiseman, Adele. *Crackpot.* Toronto: McClelland & Stewart, 1974.

Wiseman, Adele. "Goon of the Moon and the Expendables." *Malahat Review* 98 (March1992): 5-44.

Wiseman, Adele. *Memoirs of a Book-Molesting Childhood and Other Essays.* Toronto: Oxford University Press, 1987.

Wiseman, Adele. *Old Markets, New World.* Illustrated by Joe Rosenthal. Toronto: MacMillan, 1964.

Wiseman, Adele. *Old Woman at Play.* Toronto: Clarke Irwin, 1978.

Wiseman, Adele. Poems, 1981-1986. Adele Wiseman Fonds FO447, Clara Thomas Archives, Scott library, York University, 1981-92.

Wiseman, Adele. "The Dowager Empress Suite." c. 1987-1992. Adele Wiseman Fonds FO447, Clara Thomas Archives, Scott Library, York University, 1981-92.

Wiseman, Adele. *The Lovebound: A Tragi-Comedy.* c.1960. Adele Wiseman Fonds FO447. Clara Thomas Archives, Scott Library, York University.
Wiseman, Adele. *The Sacrifice.* Toronto: Macmillan, 1956.

Instructions from Poems in Progress

Never Put a Poem Off

Never put a poem off
It's a vain, capricious thing
You may put off eating
You may defer play
You may even, briefly,
Put your love away
But ask a flash of verse to wait
Till you find pencil, pen or slate
In vain,
You'll never see that joy
Made word again.

Pause

When I pause
long enough
I begin
to hear my music.
Once I begin
to hear my music
no pause
is long enough.

April 19, 1984

On the cutting room floor of consciousness

On the cutting room floor of consciousness
The fragments writhe and cry unheard,
Betrayed by the fictions above
Banished from time
They spurn the story line
And remain on principles arcane
To storm our sleep, seize the machine,
Screen themselves in our dreams
Reveal our terror, our unease
And show
There's no escape from the awful power
Of what we do not want to feel
Of what we cannot bear to know.

I CANNOT

I CANNOT BREAK FAITH
LET OTHERS DO
WHAT THEY CAN DO
LET ME DO WHAT
ONLY I CAN DO

November 4, 1984

I Cannot Be

I cannot be
The true voice of a people.
I differ from
and disagree with most.
I'll have to be
far less significant
but far more difficult,
my own true voice.

September 24, 1984

Instructions from Poems in Progress

From the very first
        "Find me"
assume the privilege of the child
adult ascendancy
the ex cathedra tone
of absolute authority.

They come in emotional code
without the verbal key.
That must be an instruction too
        "At crucial times mere words
        interfere with poetry."

+   +   +
Eggshells   owl pellets   cow dung
For that matter   masterwork   art gallery
creature itself   eventually
All disappear
We ardently muck out old middens
treasure in ancient garbage   proof
that others were here
to provide between us and raw birth
at God's fingertip   Adam's rib   Jupiter's ear
a zone to speculate

I trace the other way   haruspicate
the afterbirth of a handful of poems
for clues to how they got here,
hope next time to lure them

more swiftly through   with less pain
Each time learn better
Each time hope again

THE POEM TELLS ITSELF

Esker and drumlin, the history
of glacial thrust inferred
from passages encoded in earth's crust,
translate to fresh eyes the familiar
patterned slant of rockface, rubble,
the where and why of trough and curve
of tumbled boulder and of every pebble.

These instructions too are clues
inferred from what is graven
in the live medium my space
through which the poem tells itself
and leaves me with a shapely emptiness
that yearns to once again be scored
by yet another telling loveliness
to shape me in a new embrace.

It begins in
revelation's crucible
passionate mind.
Idea of a poem
waits on voice;
voice waits

on idea of a poem

Voice and idea
fused
in poet's heat
fulfill each other.
Poem goes off
dancing
into the typeset.

Poet blows kisses
till it's gone
Alone again, poor fool
and hooked
on continuous creation,
poet goes frantic
Hot for another one

Deeply embedded in words
fragments of rhythm beat
driving impulse throws
intuitions of meaning
more insistent
more difficult than drums

A Small Handbook
Of Working Platitudes
Collected On Discovery
That The Obvious Can Be
Surprisingly Useful

+

To discover what you want to say
you have to try to say it.

+

Not only what you want to say
but how it's said
makes what you want to say
what you want said.

+

Welcome surprises.
Ignore temptation of
the easy and familiar
They will quickly bore.
Their function I to be
discarded possibility.
Milestones, their significance
is that you pass them by.

+

Keep everything that you have done
about you as you work.
What you have rejected
you will not need to reject again,
but sometimes it contains a clue
you'll suddenly remember
a phrase, a rhythm, combination
of a rhyme or two
Abandoned sounds and junked ideas
may be signposts to alternate routes.

+

Cultivate the pleasure of rejecting.

The more rigorously you rejected,
the less you are likely
despite appearances
to be beginning anew.

+

Digressions insure inevitability.
Trace the paths which intrigue you
Be prepared to try again and again
Learn to risk the unknown track
through the wasted day. Believe
that it's there to be found. Assume
that when you find it you'll know it
the absolute route
the exemplary way.

+

Not everything is simply given
Don't let yourself deceive
Some you'd like to think's been given
you've faked, in your eagerness to receive.
Beware, especially, the false perfection
of the second hand epiphany.

+

At any point take comfort
but not too much
from what you have already done.
You've not completely made a good beginning
until you have made a good end.

+

Be patiently
prepared to celebrate
completion of your labours
only to begin again

repeatedly.

+

Always obey dissatisfaction.
The greatest uncertainty
is not in the setting out
but in the moment before completion.
The moment of most intense dissastisfaction
precedes the miraculous synthesis.

+

You should always be surprised by the end result.
It's the moment when you learn what you've been about.

+

Do not resent time spent.
The final poem
no matter how strenuously won
is always given.

+

Later, when the poem's done
stands integral and alone
I linger in the mental field
still fingering the way it felt,
get caught in the precipitate
as all these mysteries translate
around the one that got away,
soak in the rain of afterwords,
Feel like a critic, out of it
awash in findings and afraid
in all that flood of smugly connected words
my new instruction, the very first

"Find me"
will choose to refuse to make itself heard.

In Our Play

Loved one
You said you would call
Again
Should I
Hold my breath
Again?
                    July 23, 1982

We should have been lovers
These three years past.
We'll never make up for it, never
But oh to begin at last
                    December 11, 1983

Eyes meet, you smile

I dream a taut wire,
My heart
Funambulates a dance,
Mad pirouette
From eye to aye,
Wills my glad fall
To your lips net,
Will heart in mouth
To mouth.

You glance aside,
Snap wire. Heart drops.
No lips to break
The plunge of that deep ache.

Till sudden life, your smile
I fly,
Heart wills forevers
Now,
Strips pain, risks all
And dives.

This turbulence,
This blue, this drowning deep,
Your eyes.

Oh I admire the ease
With which your glance
Can engineer
My fall,
My rise.

June 14, 1981

The silent telephone

The silent telephone
always about to burst
into true love

You enter. I try

You enter. I try
to glance aside
but my eyes catch, dig in.
I hang helplessly
on your every movement
riveted by
those greedy crabs
my eyes.

Touching you, once, my fingertip thought

Touching you, once, my fingertip thought,
How can this be? How can there be
a forehead like this? Eyelid, lash frill,
gesture of cheekbone, sudden fine thread
around thrill of silk lip?
Bliss of your skin is the question still
Etched on my fingertip.

This strange invasion

This strange invasion,
sudden blaze of six and six red wings,
dreams of truant angels, sighs
of concupiscent seraphim
enthralled by the green flicker of your eyes.

Hush

Hush, it's a gift my beloved,
Receive it with awe, tenderly;
You who believe there was no room
In your life for me,
See how much larger our lives
Were intended to be.

November 21, 1982

In our play

In our play
performance of the parts
is always touching

Entre acts
we build the mood
to feel the parts
grow with the play

In the climax of our play
the parts come
together

Experience, it seems

Experience, it seems,
affects the expectations,
not the dreams

Rhymed Primal

Eve and Adam kiss,
Taste innocent wedded bliss,
Hear a little hiss.

A good part of the art

A good part of the art
of self defense
is to survive
what you are learning.

My nemesis has been
the back that kills
by turning.

We register degree of hurt

We register degree of hurt
by something in the cry,
Through echoes, sound the deep.
But nothing in my yell
can tell of the continued fall
as well as your long silence plumbs
in me, precisely, depths of this abyss,
the pitched intensity of my emotion,
your recoil.

Without You

Winter passed without you
Spring found me
looking for a self delusion
on which to base a summer's hope.
I have not far left to fall.

June 25, 1984

You Can Come Out Now

Don't be uneasy, loved one.
Look, you can see it's done
I am alone
Love is gone.
There is nothing to fear here, loved one,
The murder of love leaves no stains.
Only the sweetness remains
Only the sweetness remains.

I'll tell you something, loved one,
Love died but I heard it say,
Somewhere there are real people
Who don't behave this way,
When you bring your love to real people
They don't say, "Take it away."

You can come out now, loved one,
Love is gone.
Don't be uneasy, loved one,
Look, you can see it's done.
I am alone
Love is gone.
There is nothing to fear here, loved one,
The murder of love leaves no stains
Only the sweetness remains
Only the sweetness remains.

July 17, 1983

Haiku: In Your Garden

In your garden my
small, pink, bleeding heart survives
your indifference.

How many lovers driven

How many lovers driven   driven
to curse   to curse
what isn't given   isn't given
cannot replace   cannot replace
what they would even   would even cursing
embrace   embrace

There Is Magic

Surely, there is magic, and
alchemy, the force
of unseen powers,
harnessed, pulling in directions
contrary, gravitational,
magnetic forces, tugging,
unseen, realigning lives,
spoiling, rearranging
capricious unseen.
Why else would I, unchoosing and
unchosen, love you and
choose to love you still.

A Fragile Status Quo

A fragile status quo depends
On our convention that we both pretend
I neither know what I am saying
when I tell you that I love you,
nor that you hear,
and in my fear
that if I forget myself
and reach out to touch,
you'll ring down curtains
on the offending suppliant
who comes too near.

Hence, the scene is set with you and me
chatting amiably.
Your mild discomfort is offset
by my determination to amuse,
and I ignore the care
with which your glance avoids
the traps of hope
set by my eyes.

My hunger, the involuntary
witchcraft of desire
makes palpable the thickened air
between us, as my eyes
slide down your lowered lids
and over the soft flush
of your embarrassed cheeks.
How could I love you more

than to submit, these many weeks
to this most subtle
violation of the flesh,
my arms obediently still
against their will,
my dense, infatuated spirit
reaching for the dream of your embrace?

March 6, 1982

In My Notebook

Fresh thrill after long absence
You living in my notebook still
This love keeps well in language
That I try with words to kill.

November 8, 1982

Send Not Regrets

Send not regrets because you cannot love me
There is no debt where love is gladly spent
I am your debtor reckoned truly
Love's grateful player and love's instrument.

The mean accuse their loves of making magic
If you've bewitched me mine is all the gain
I saw you and my body turned to music
And music is my antidote to pain.

I'd vainly sought in things and thought well being
But simple source of joy in you have found
Love given freely ends by freeing
Surrender wholly and be wholly sound.

Though you deny us harmony of hearts
I'll bless you in the singing of my parts.

It's winter now

It's winter now
What shall I do
With all this love gone stale?

Throw it to the birds.

But how survive
without love's crumbs
this deadly winter within?

Let the birds in.

Love is fed to need
feeds life to love
The strengthening of wings

Requital brings.

Mysteries of Flight

Currents

For Tamara

Those of us who fly
know currents,
learn tricks from birds,
the skill to navigate
the invisible,
take off into the wind.

We who swim
read currents on the skin,
know pull of tides
and tug of undertow,
learn limits of the thrill
of mastery.

Who know the world
ride shifting currents
learn to balance
in capricious flow,
learn to look as though
we're going where we want to go.

We dreamers are seized
by subterranean currents,
navigate blind

alleys of the mind
know the unbuttoned universe
of flux and fears between the ears.

Lovers, we learn to feel
equations of emotion, know
how to make one
in searing current's fusion, know
we're briefly current and done, but oh
Who stepped up the current so?

I have been daring in my time,
have flown, swum, navigated blind,
and know the salmon's desperate wisdom.
To assure tomorrow, love for you,
I would to my own current's end
against all currents go.

February 22, 1982

Birds Burst

Birds burst from purple brush
catapult into sky
great flocks of birds that fly
like snapping fingers

Haiku Recipe

Fresh blue glass of sky
One half slice of pallid moon
Taste of night at noon.

Mysteries of Flight

By day
the sky slicing gulls
gather light

The ragged
ripping bats
concentrate the night

Massed starlings

Massed starlings in flight
Complex rhythms of
their shuttle flow in space
Random must be
most intricate of dances.

Some music

Some music
like the wind   whistling
in the aching little bones of birds.

Summer Sunsets: Backyard Toronto

I

Loud trees their blackening leaves
in surge like distant surf
wash down the sands of sunset
with glowing pools of green

II

Flight of seagulls, breasts ablaze, draw eyes
across a cloud of dusty rose
Horizon glows pale yellow and pale green.
Sun setting fires the leafy oak,
burns golden core, leaves copper coals
and one small bird with burnished breast
pours molten song from dying furnace of stoked light.

III

The last long lingering kiss of sun
has pinked the chubby cloud and turned
the oak deep copper, wine and blackened green.
The bumbleflight of bats begins.
I hear them chirping in the smoky blue
see their wings flutter, herding insects,
gathering their supper in.

Standards

Every evening I judge the sunset
from where I sit,
And when it's what folks call a beauty, a gasper
I'm hardest on it.
All this outrageous colour,
this vulgar show,
the extravagant way the setting sun
just lets itself go;
That bright blaze of orange
those purples, those melodramatic greens
are tawdry, excessive, crass,
like paintings in the five and dime,
Let's face it,
Nature has no class.

I hear the birds

I hear the birds
peeping holes in the dark
to let in the dawn.

Summer Sun: Autumn Rain

Jewelled children in the sun
line the edge of swimming pool
wet   atremble   daring freighted
for the inner order poised
to break loose   step out   hold nose
drop sudden   one by one

Dully silver   seeping day
matching tears in gleaming rows
line the undersides of twigs
small bright jewels   plumply weighted
break their crystal necklaces
drop sudden   one by one

Found Haiku from Tamara's Cry

Ahhh, I just saw all
of that poppy's petals fall.
One by one they fell.

Autumn Haiku

Leaves leave after rain
imprint of captured shadows,
Pavement remembers.

Astonished by the season's politics

Astonished by the season's politics
the banished bumble bee
drones urgent revolutions in the dying flowers
who nod, nudged by agent provocateur the breeze.
Smiling nature, time inexorable
turn their children in.

Ascent

Ascent is sheer delight,
but sudden birds must face
a danger of return
so swift it baffles flight.
And there, you'd think,
is where the skill comes in
to brake the dive
but neither reflexes
nor timing can control
the throttle grip
of your hand on my heart
or my tailspin.
The perilous moment
for all high flyers
is the descent.

December 6, 1982

The acrobatic autumn leaves

The acrobatic autumn leaves
flip and flow
Down they go
like little boys
all for show.

Haiku: Fly Out of Season

Fly out of season
buzzing in my window, dies
down like wind-up toy.

Grey autumn days

Grey autumn days
Repel illusion.
In silver light the leaves
already turned
hang from the trees unlit,
are what they are
limp and rain ragged,
no longer seem to put
so gay a face on death.

Autumn Days

Autumn days
the messy time of year
the time I'm most of home in,
trees half undressed
in the disheveled bedroom of no world,
reluctant to part with their leaves this year
stayed stubbornly green
and even thought it's late
the season still plays
a slow strip tease
through lingering autumn days,

drawing the notes of colour out,
each leaf its moment
the long cadenza that modulates the oak
through variations orange and green
to rusty russet rustlings,
bitter chocolate sun gilded,
subtle hum of shadings in-between
that binds the scene.

The hectic stages of decline
performed at last,
each stem is bitten off,
leaves parachute to grass,

lie cupping light in curling plumby
many fingered old men's hands
brown veined and leathery and dry
till rain, relaxing rigor mortis, straightens them
for me to marvel at their elegant design.

December 19, 1983

Spaces

Spaces

It's not the words the danger's in, it's in
the drops between, it's in the spaces of the dream
we fall, the danger's in the print, the way we trust
ourselves to structure on the page, believe
in guy wires taut with rhythms caught, safe nets
of springing rhyme. What mind's short reach can long
hold swinging words, hold slippery thoughts?
In the recurring dream the child's alone
High on suspended footbridge to the city park.
Spaces gape between collapsing boards,
The cataract's below, she clings to swinging ropes,
and mommy and the sandwiches are gone
and Tarzan's busy elsewhere saving Jane.
Write how mum held your forehead as you puked
out of the window of the old streetcar. Write
of the park the zoo the elms the feasts laid on
the living green. Write how you later missed
the sturdy bridge now concrete low on sluggish stream
and write how terror gathers in the spaces
and the fall is a recurring dream.

August 28, 1986

The Gifted Itch Scratcher

A tribute

We who have known unreachable itch revere
the Gifted Itch Scratcher, who has divined
that simply to scratch and be done
is never enough, for a careless scratch
is to the itch more maddening than none.
An itch is complex, elusive, hard to locate,
to define precisely and with exactitude, alleviate.
The Gifted Scratcher of Itches has the touch,
is sensuous and with a taste for symbiosis,
generous in the enjoyment of another's pleasure,
leaves no itch unscratched of itching hide,
and will not let even imagined itch remain unsatisfied.

July 4, 1983

Friendship

Ugly, ugly ugly the night
you soaked our friendship in alcohol
and set it alight.

April 2, 1982

Typewriter Blues

By the pricking of my thumbs
Carpal tunnel syndrome
This way comes.

March 14, 1984

Instructions Found on the Deceased

You will run
in progressively smaller circles
till you're all that's left.
Exit through yourself.

November 18, 1983

Impossible

Impossible
If you have any sanity in you
Not to be a little mad.

August 18, 1984

Ancestor

Behind my inability
to bow my head silently
accept received ideas
with which I disagree.
I sense the furnace blast,
The fire-tempered hide
Of my ancestor Avrom
The first iconoclast.

June 13, 1984

History Lesson

Jews who long to shine in the gentile world
must learn to shine in the gentile way
Heine learned the great price of ambition
Wherever he turned to be was not to be
The ticket of admission is complicity.
Heine, once he understood, returned
but left an unexpected glow
even in the gentile world.

April 10, 1985

Mopping Up

Biographers papering over closets
Gentiles expunging traces of Jews
Men ignoring the story of women
Newspapers censoring the news
History one long mopping up process
Aimed at erasing alternate voices.

December 14, 1983

The Nascent Evil

That nascent evil against which
you will not raise your voice today,
tomorrow, fully grown,
won't let you raise your head.

October 31, 1983

River of Time

The river of time
may be an illusion
but we drown in it anyway.

December 21, 1984

As I Write the Words Down

As I write the words down
I feel such love for them.
Mama sorting her buttons
and bits of cloth
to find her dolls.

December 12, 1983

My Mother Must Have Dreamed

My mother must have dreamed
through all her life of loving us
those other dreams that women dream, of love.
My father, gentle soul, walled in
paid out his lifetime for his family
but lived in his soliloquy.
I still remember mystery, unease
and learning, late in adolescence
that to spare us children
they saved all their quarrels
for the bedroom late at night.,
imagine hearing in my sleep
their hissing in the mentholated air,
try to imagine kissing but remember
mother blurting once, when I was grown,
my father never understood
could never grope his way to tenderness.
I think of Hamlet, sensitive, obtuse,
imagining the nunnery
alternative to his brisk use.
I think my mother must have dreamed
of love. Yet over half a century
"He was my friend," she said, when father died,
"I've lost a friend." And oddly in the end,
my father came to her in dreams.

April 9, 1985

What Is the Night?
A Fancy for Children

What is the night?
Dark bird at rest
Fluffed out over her brood, her nest,

Where does night go?
Condensed like dew
star embedded
the starlings flew.

Each little bird
a flying nest
tired stars rocking
to daylight rest.

Where is the moon?
Bright eye of night
will sometimes stay
to watch the light.

Great golden bird
whose eye is sun
awake the world
to day begun.

Earth's creatures stretch
and fledglings grow.

Pale moon's amazed
how colours glow.

Where does day go?
Night spreads its wings.
Day shuts its eye
like all tired things

July 29, 1985

The Void

The Void before, Death stalking me behind,
yet I must move, and where I enter
Emptiness escapes, flees me
as I flee my pursuer.
Led, fled and haunted all my days
For awhile I fancied emptiness afraid
of my vitality. Once, in my youth,
I even boasted, "Hold there, what's the Void to me?
What's Death? Scavengers beyond the compass
of my fire's bright light? The subject
and the object of my life, the value
must be me."

Now in my rushing middle age
with Death drawn closer, I perceive
the Void foreshortened at my edge of days,
and Emptiness so near she leaves Her breath behind,
perceive myself a pawn, as in some lover's game,
perceive myself transparent. See,
She runs and He pursues; She hides, He seeks,
She flirts before me; from behind, He peeks,
and finally, She tires.

The time will come
that where I enter, Emptiness will stay,
that I will enter Emptiness,
that Death will enter Her through me.

I am the life They brought along
to be the witness to Their play.
They let me grow into my space
and ripen to Their appetite.
I am Their blanket and Their picnic lunch,
Their toy, Their gull, Their decoy and Their trysting place.

June 11, 1984

The Dowager Empress Suite

The Death of the Emperor

The birds have left their gilded cages
left the Emperor (his rages
legendary) left
his eunuchs in despair.   Save in trees they tease
those buxom fellows pleading   Swoop
to make them futile leap and clutch
out of reach they soar
with shriek and giggle
in the pleasure of their element.

Mischievous angels shed their dross,
splatter erstwhile keepers now
who brush pied smears distraught
to clownish stains.   In tears
beseech exquisite favourites
all jokes aside, alight, ere
news of naughty escapade reach ear
of Emperor and all the court
His Anger Absolute must bear.

Alas those fowl are having too much fun.
The disrespect of their reply,
the irresponsibility
presumption they know better
than their betters, their assumption
wings give them the right to fly.

The whole uncivil shrill cacophony
has brought the Emperor whose temper's

leash has lately been a mere
abbreviation of its celebrated short
since somewhat short of his anointed lease
(ten thousand years) his Majesty's
been feeling out-of-sorts, and subject
to absurdly mortal fears.

And here the merest of his subjects,
pets, His Toys have occupied
his middle air
without a by-your-leave
and colonize his sky,
Oh heads indeed shall fly;

But all his eunuchs prudent fled,
are hiding under (the last place he's
likely to go) his Empress's bed.
Arrows, stinging birds in unison twang
shimmering bolts of feather plummet
blood splatters the Emperor's gown.

The archers draw again   again,
great sinewy hand are sore
yet their Master cries for more,
for if mere birds can shake
the balance of ten thousand years
What, when the rabble hears?

The Emperor's kettle whistles shrill
his blood is on the boil
And of a sudden his fluid spouts

from mouth and noise and eyes and ears
as the Emperor shorts
his ten thousand years.

He lies in a gold and azure heap
with stains of blackening red on his robes
and streaking crimson streams
starring out of empurpled face.
He is ringed by a gory brocade
Of arrow bristling angels fall

Blood and arrows are quickly gone,
The Emperor's vestments are spotless
The intemperate years erased from his face
The scene rearranged a picture tableau
Refined to a solemn decorum.

And then the invited rabble arrives
To rearrange its memories
The rabble with little children's eyes
hears that when the Emperor died
his favourite birds of one mind Chose
to follow him to Paradise.

The rabble cheers, one mind one throat
though some shed tears, and some take note
and shrug. As Emperors go he goes
at the going rate. What next?
In these affairs of state the best
a serf can do is mindless shout,
anticipate traditional handout.

One sun goes down, another rises,
by god, this one a daughter, there's
a joke, goes down a sun comes up
a daughter. Don't laugh no, eyes everywhere,
ha ha, ten thousand years a bitch.

The Rule of the Dowager

The Empress is led
through formalities of grief
as through a fog.
Attentive ears are screwed
to her every nuance of breath.
She is heard to murmur, "I have been
too long asleep." Eyebrows are raised,
eyes meet.   In each head
her utterance instantly gutted
and red, like the entrails of fowl, pronounced
a Wise Enigma by some, by others
Astutely Oblique.   Still others
recall the Flighty Princess wed
by fiat of Emperor to vassal Prince
Fit to rule and Empire and a foolish girl.

Well, what's wisdom now?
To vie with the rest
for the Dowager's ear, eyes keen
to assess her perpendicular
and guess in whose direction she will lean
and what the blandishments for which she'll fall.

She is half-drowned in good advice
from ministers who offer her relief
from petty household chores of Empire.

At last she speaks "Know that if need be We
will council take and humbly heed the wise,
But like Our late lamented spouse
in all these years We shared this throne,
We will rule alone."

She Punishes the Birds

Her first decrees,
touching the defection
that has plunged an Empire into grief
Fit punishment for birds
is banishment
Banishment from gilded cages
Banishment from sybaritic pleasures,
Banishment henceforth to middle air
to take their chances in the trees.
Let them see what it's like
to have to fly, come cold come warm
to fend for themselves come wet come dry,
by the tug of their beaks
to earn their worms
from hard unyielding clay.
They will yet come creeping back
on knobbed arthritic claws
to lament with their shivering progeny
the Paradise that was.

"Nor will they find Us adamant"
Her Majesty avers
"but as with long lost kin
recovered, Our delight
in their return will be
to see them free to share
the dangers and the rights
as equal citizens each in her kind
of earth as well as air."

She Punishes the Eunuchs

Coaxed from beneath her bed
who'd oft in secret hid
to entertain
recumbent Majesty
with spicy tidbits thought
by Emperor and Court
to her unknown,
the Empress stern
her eunuchs judges
derelict, condemned to live
as birds their erstwhile keepers
in costumes and in song
by art transformed
fair substitute for fowl
to entertain the Court.

"There will be no more eunuchs
manufactured here, " she vows.
"For future song there will be women who
though not by science modified,
if given voice, will do."

Courtiers and counselors
fishmouthing their ears
in first astonishment
at this new reign,
now carp in earnest, try

to gather deep in secret pools
to bubble their unease
but everywhere discover
eunuchs, duty this time
passionately serving. Not
an arras nor a nook to hide
but appear they will
in gaudy all fantastical
to warble and to trill.

The Rendezvous of the Courtiers

Cruel, spurring horses
hard and fast they ride
to meet in hidden woods
and guarded mountain passes
Outrage not to be contained
at ancient rights denied
of private sport, at public
mockery in double travesty
Of what was meant to be.
Robbed of their birds
and of fresh eunuchs too!

How swift heroic age
of Emperors has passed.
Once, even slaves could secretly
with guile and kill superior
entrap and tame
the poorest man entrepreneur
behind His Lordship's back afford
the dream of birds galore
pale tender breasts and sticky thighs
and feathered beds and meat for holidays
with bones and heads and giblets fit for soup
and brains to suck.   Oh put to work
a bird or two or three
domesticate in golden ages past
and meanest men aristocrats became
of cottage industry.

Their Lordships reminisce, extol
the courage and the trapper's skill
of poachers they once, apprehending
mercilessly flayed, Seek comfort
in the brotherhood of men by birds
and by caprice of Dowager betrayed
More than ever are in love
with romance of the lure and snare
with variations of the mating call
and hypnotize each other
faute de mieux, with lengthy
catalogues of injury sustained
from fragile birds and brainless
who eschew strong arms
of their protectors,
and by Dowager empowered choose
loose living in the skies
and endlessly extol
in youth corrupting melody
deplored by wise philosophy
the pleasures of their own autonomy.

Young bucks aristocratic visit
huts of expert poachers
plan campaigns to lure from flight
renegade delight, promise servants
large reward for silent aid, offer
second dibs at lesser fowl
for complicity

brute survival, which for poor man
is the kiss of history

Imitative flutings
and abandoned dancing
of the rainbow feather-boa-d
flying eunuchs of the Court
with a following they sense
with joy is all their own
can feel their audience respond
and zeal surpassing judgment
daringly they tease
Audacious choose to dance in cages
winning turbulent applause
while the Empress sits impassive
till her silence gives them pause.

Yet the Empress Is
Inordinately Fond
of Story and of Song

She summons bards and troubadours,
musicians fabulists
historians philosophers
comedians and chroniclers
alchemists dramatists
astrologers and oracles
all sundry liars welcoming,
Plies them with questions
and with comments strange
The Court grown used
to utterance ineffable
from sybilline Celestial
Imperial Incumbent, even greets
deliberate absurdities
with ecstacies of "Oh your Majesty!"s

She smiles and thinks of leaping over walls
and floating sunlike in her yellow robes
through all the kingdoms
searching out at last
one bard who knows
unfinished tale her life has heard.
She is sick of Princesses she
never knew, by wicked witches
put to sleep suspended years, who
wakened by the kiss of handsome Prince
assume the happy every after
while the Court polite applauds.

Her Majesty retires alone
to chamber of the painted birds
and rails at mirrors and at walls,
"What of the Prince
who finds his bride awake and lively,
filled with vivid life?
Whose first instruction is
'Sit still, you will upset my horse,'
Who bends her days inexorable
to the very shape of sleep
those long suspended hears.
Time is the kiss
She wakens to, transformed, a Witch."
The Witch Who Rules and Must

Forbid her son's adventuring
to punish for some slight her son-in-law
whose tributary kingdom he suspects
is ready to encroach upon his own.

An Empire for a nursery
and he on slaughter bent
dares the very air to breathe
while daughter, once a lively girl
has settled down, sits side-saddle
in favour, buoyed by run of luck
that has produced all heirs
for her ambitious Prince
Regrets the Empress interferes
in politics. Her lord
must do what He must do
Scold rather brother's airs imperial

His hand, since mother banished
hawk from wrist, has nothing better
to do it seems, than twist and turn
with ambitious schemes.

Why can't the children get along?

The Tower of Celestials

Scrubbed and purified, sequestered
from all human taint, unseen
beneath her panoply of veils
the sunbright Queen of Empire
obeys the yearly ritual
that justifies her days
is carried by the Empire's finest bred
each honoured beyond dreams
all gorgeously arrayed
to enter and to tread the holy stairs
and bear their own Celestial
to pleas and win their yearly weal
from those great Gods Her Kin.

The gaping hordes whipped back
fall sighing to heir knees and wait.

Within, the silent process winds
around and round the rising walls
where no external sound can reach
and each if not preoccupied
with base design
can feel the presence
near of the Divine.

They have reached the final stair
her escort kneels, averted eyes
that cannot face the sudden
shaft

of light, her jeweled blaze
as Majesty descends her chair,
ascends, is drawn rather, beyond
what can be borne by human gaze.

No sooner is she gone
and once again the shaft of light
illuminates the way
her erstwhile escort, cloaks flung back
and daggers drawn,
swarm silent the forbidden stairs
nor pause before the praying Queen
Each strikes with fervor through
Her robes voluminous, and swift
they heave her up and over
crenellated wall, their leader crying,
"Majesty, free as your birds, you fly!"

From below, as from a single voice,
a gasp, a wail as tiny brilliant
growing sun comes toppling from the tower
splatters on the cobbles
Blood sun reddened at the core

And while the hordes still frozen kneel
sudden in their midst appears a troop
Its Head, another sun,
so brilliantly caparisoned and matched
his horse alone could pass for one sun more

And from the Tower rush conspirators
to kneel, their hands still gory
at his horse's feet.
Them he spears through.

Scarce has the rabble indrawn breath
when from the palace gates
an army issues
and on palace balcony
another sun appears   The Empress
Dowager sees faithful eunuch in
her image image brutally undone and
ready dressed to take her place
her son, who sees his fortune's coin
in mid-flight spin, and quick as ever cries
to the companions of his enterprise
to storm the Palace and prevail
against the capons and their hen,
and die as men.   He leads the charge
before his half an army falls away
and he is halfway up with bloodied sword,
the sweeping stairs where he played soldier
as a boy and now as then his mother
waits and listens, wonders idly
will he come alone
or once again command someone to pluck
his triumph and his shame
and swiftly do away the doer
with the blame   She waits
and all grows silent on the stairs
and still she cannot move
but like some jeweled insect

from all sides beset
is frozen visible
when finally her son
in arms of an old officer
with courage more than most
is to his mother
for the last time borne.

Still the cobbles
Still the square
Still the pious hordes
too dazzled by
too many suns to run
incidental to the rages
of the great they lie
intimate among the fallen
blood with blood at last commingled
Trust a poor man's luck!

The Empress Disappears
Into the Legends of her Reign

Respect that's sown
in blood soaked terrain
Flowers prodigies
Swift flies her fame
with growing rumour
as it rounds the rolling world
Far and wide the story is received
of an Empress who has eaten
of her sons, for proof
she suffers none but only sons
of aristocracy to taste her food,
who regularly disappear.
This Empress to the grief
of lovers of good sport
has elevated birds to be
her ministers and spies
In consequence there's none
in all that mighty empire dares
to speak in counterwise, for fear
of flying accusations, swallows
robins, sparrows, starlings tits,
the juicy breasted partridge,
teasing nightingale, the throaty dove
that oh too constant voice of love
that drives men mad
from sheer monotony, all all
the enemy
by Royal Sorceress empowered
to guard the middle air

birds cannibal who intercept
and gobble up, prevent
all access to the gods
of human prayer.

The Witch employs auxiliary
a race of eunuchs
for her services unmanned
her most ferocious warriors
in victory frustrate
of keenest joys of spoils of war
tear from defeated and their dead
instead that which themselves they lack
on which they grisly feast
with their mad Sovereign and her birds
to celebrate the downfall of all foes
who dare to penetrate that Empire rich
as it is vast to profitably free
with holy warfare her benighted subjects
from their evil yoke

What Can Harm an Empress
Who Has Lived
Ten Thousand Years a Day?

Sometimes she consults with
that old officer
who alone has seen her weep,
is always grateful for advice
she as gratefully ignores
as she ignores his surliness
regards him well
And when he pleads the need
To build a navy worthy
of Her Empire to discourage
strangers predatory
she agrees and now sits lofty
of a summer's day ensconced
on sumptuous appointed deck
of regal marble vessel
This her Navy, new
in gardens of her summer palace
overlooking water-lilied lake
and entertains her daughter
who, till recently asleep
her children grown
is now arounds and baffled
and on frequent visits urged
by her ambitious princeling
snxious to ensure succession
gradually thaws, confides her pain
and weeping finds again her mother

in the Empress and the balm
of laughter shared
and strength that can afford to know
what she has had to learn
to earn her life awake,
the arcane truths of every day
for which the witches burn

The Dowager Is Not Allowed
by That Old Officer
to Scant Her Reckoning

She is logical as dreams to him
as jokes of children as the wife who waits
at home in comfort stoking obscure rage
Them he can dismiss. She dismisses here.
But he knows naught if not his duty
takes his life in hand and speaks
"The tax which is levied and collected
should have built a navy
to bring honour to Your Empire
has impoverished the people further
Everywhere they die of hunger
and for what?"
Having spoken he attends her rage,
Court medicine traditional
for troubled mind revealed unwelcome
is the nod of Monarch
followed by the stroke of axe.
The Empress nods.

"Henceforth whene'er a poor man dies
he is to have a hero's funeral
full naval honours
and a public declaration
he has faithful served
Our interests at sea."
So saying, to his great astonishment
The sun breaks on the Dowager's averted face
Her smile is history

The poor of that great realm
No longer have a word for Death.
'Smile of the Dowager' it's called
when your turn's up.   A hero's end
does something for the rabble
life has never done
Gives them illusions of the rich
the meanest beggar
Hero to his Queen
And Death so prodigal is celebrated here
as never on the battlefield.   The poor
the horses, the rabble
have become an aristocracy
of kind, develop airs, anticipate
the heroes they must be
and are the envy of all poverty.

Indeed the poor of alien lands
en masse have taken walking stick
and cup in hands, whole families
the sick and dying too,
who drag themselves
through swamps and jungle, torrents blizzards
over alps and deserts
braving beasts and goblins.
Failed and fallen litter
the periphery of Empire
Bare survivors swarming

Overpower border guards
To prove they're citizens ere falling
and are trampled by more future heroes still

When the keepers of Her coffers
nervously suggest this
celebrating death
among the poor unending
strains the budged
Majesty is heard to murmur
"Surely cheaper far
than sending them to war."

Petition of the Aging Eunuchs

Her eunuchs as they age perceive
how all around them multiply
Can scarcely now remember once
it seems ten thousand years ago
they were elate that none henceforth
would be capricious mutilate.
They own enduring value
without issue is at issue here
and even all that pain endured
of deprivation and as sport
of cruel court, nostalgia
time's great traitor bathes in sunset glow.
Who will be as loyal
or as supple to her Royal uses
once they're gone? This they please
in suit insistent proving
meanest in the world have issue
which to them alone denied
could by gesture of their Empress
generous be rectified.
There are so many children of the poor.
What's a little pain felt by
a likely little beggar set against
career, success, a life of service
to the Empress of the Greater World?

"If Majesty would but restore
that ancient custom   place it

in our hands alone, hereditary
Sons, our heirs of choice created
in Her service would
perpetuate our line."

Petition of the Paupers

Her starving poor   heads now held high
with vision now perceive the skies
are riotous with possibilities
of winged roasts
of broilers boilers fryers stews
of flying barbecues
eggs coddled   omelettes and sunny eyed
or fried on horseback   menus succulent
Protected by the Queen's decree
from the assault of cutlery

All these as favored by her Majesty
Alive as her impoverished
Heroic grave-locked hallowed
pseudo sailors are
in hollow bellied Death.   'Tis insult
even to a pauper's dignity
to be thus rated lesser
live than merest fowl
They, newly proud with awkward phrase
Petition sovereign in all things wise
Name birds in death Heroic Wings
of the Imperial Navy
and let the starving poor
them honour in the feasting
Thus the poor would self-abolished
in the eating be reborn
with bellies full

as frolicsome as any flow
and more than any fit to rule
unruly fowl, as having been themselves
most ruled and eager
to extend the benefit of their
experience, what good is learning else?

Eye of Empress

What is the cage with bird again
(though eye of Empress everywhere)
who nests and lays and sleeps
and dreamy nibbles gilded bars?
'Twas from this very cage
that broody gravid goose
all unsuspecting one bright day
still dreaming golden gosling worlds
and gorged with gild of gilded bars
meandered forth, the snowy summit
of her kind, the Midas bird
all innocence and generosity
who little knew she never would return

See where she waddles followed by
The tearbursts of a weeping sun
That blinding splash on golden eggs
Oh fated bird! Vain violence of man!
With what impatient greed fowl merger done
to motherhood and mystery
Had seemly reverence but stayed the axe
full many generations had been spared
the brutish legend of her tragic fate
and we this much delayed denouement
that it was all, poor innocent,
in what she ate

For this the eye of Empress never sleeps
For this her eagle image scours the skies

And when that shepherd lad goes boldly
at his Lord's behest, and dares to climb
the sheerest crag to rob the eagle's nest
all for the promise of a noble lady
bird to call his own, and by that raging
eagle is discovered and flung down
they swear the very heavens heard him shriek
before the baleful eye
the rush of that ferocious beak
"Eye of the Empress!" Although some
with hearing less acute,
who saw him, briefly, fly,
heard only "Eyeeeeeee!"

They tell it still
with sideways glances meaningful
how swiftly consummates
prompt vulture
that ignoble bird
Her gory victory in Eagle's guise
and further how
the burning Eye
of Empress everywhere prevents
the gentle helpless Birds
their choices free who must perforce
Caged in protective custody
be hidden from the jealous Eye
and Her unspeakable revenge

Quarrels in Waiting

Her daughter's Potentate in waiting
nicknamed "Almost" Emperor has long
his Future Power overdrawn
He stomachs ill slow souring
of despotic dreams while Dowager
lives on, can almost hear the snickers
of his fellow kings
as he ages in the wings
Is grown afraid of even his own sons
who gad about, win jousts and tourneys
Everywhere stir longings languorous
to flutter feather hearts of Royal Maids
and with their fathers make alliances
unholy, while his Queen returned again
from visit to the Empress
cheerily reports anew
that Mother for her age
and her responsibilities
is wondrous spry.

Does she secretly commend
her sons to the old woman
smooth the way for one or other
to play leapfrog over father?

Brooding, he erupts with narrowed eyes
and freighted utterance, that

wives who too much spoil
their sons, Her brother's case in point,
will live to bury them.

Her bones melt on the instant thought
She dare not show her gelid dread
but smiles instead
that little smile he has begun to hate.

Come to think of it he can't remember
when she last assured him
She would never want to rule like mother

Death of an Empress

"What will become of us?" they cry,
What country can survive without its poor?
What comity without its prayer?
What citizen without control of some
small lesser destiny to mark his rung above?
And what aggression greater or more subtle
than to shake the very ladder
she's supposed to lie beneath and prop.
What power to engender fear,
The old witch undermines the world we want
to know.   In nations
indignation grows, and men
experience again familiar
nervous irritation that precedes
the massive haemorraging of menses
they call war.
And march they must.

For want of shorter passage
to the distant Empire rich
They go clanking over lawns
of neighbours and collecting tribute
volunteers involuntary
and that rich patina of adventure
and of hardship overcome
that will be so irresistible
to youthful second wives.

Finally they reach and penetrate

the Empire, find it everything
they hoped for and they feared,
an Empire balanced n the cusp of chaos
for an instant strangely lovely, strangely
possible and scary, and an instant
later by their swords restored
to sane administration,
unimaginably rich
for some few takers
in the victor's tangible rewards

Strangely querulous and ancient
those most vaunted vicious eunuchs
disaffected by their Queen's refusal
of some trivial request
And her poor, though elevated,
discontent with none below to kick.

As for birds, they're not at all bad
Once they're tagged and lessons learned
swift return to their best nature
and in eagerness to please, will sing
only when they're sung to, now
clip each other's wings.

Back at last to normal
Carnage, pillage, insurrections,
despots, wars, complaints
unhappiness and discontent
all the old familiar rhythms
in their places, briefly, permanence

But they never got the Empress
They got something but
she wasn't what they thought
And it took some fighting first.
This old officer was stationed
at the closed door of her chamber
and he slew so many there
before they hacked him up
They had to climb up squishing
over all their comrades' bodies,
didn't take the time to shove them over
Everyone wanted to get at her first
past the freshly splattered door of ivory
inlaid that opened to their shove
They tumbled in
And there she was
for all their furor waiting silently
It stopped them just to see her there

She sat with such serenity
her multiple millennia,
For an instant their own presence
was in doubt, which they dispelled
with a great shout of triumph
fell on her with no preliminaries
(as she wasn't young)
their heat all in their swords
their hate spurred by the words
that foamed out from their mouths.

They tore her open.
They ripped her apart.

They hacked and they slashed, how the feathers flew!
But the blood didn't flow, only feathers
The Empress had nothing but feathers
within, nothing but feathers stuffed in her
skin, Feathers, all feathers feathers only
They hacked and they slahed and they raged
that she had somehow unmanned and
escaped them, made them feel silly
in chamber grown thick and thicker
with feathers, like nothing more
than the room at night
of children after a pillow fight.

Her substance divided
her essence multiplied, she fills their mouths
and flied up their noses. Coughing,
spewing, slashing blind, they ground her feathers
only with the sodden weight
of each others' blood
Nor do they cease their manly labours
till they have hacked each other
beyond reflection.

Deep in the place where the Empire was
a cult exists of birds
who worship the Dowager Empress in feathers
believe when you sneeze her voice is blessing you
and know she will always be there
where you lay your egg at night
and hatch your dreams.

Elsewhere, fear of the Dowager Empress persists.

Notes

Introduction

"Doing the worst possible thing for the best reason" in "The Permissible and the Possible: Adele Wiseman," *Lives & Works: Interviews by Bruce Meyer and Brian O'Riordan* (Windsor, ON: Black Moss Press, 1992) 118-127.

See *Selected Letters of Margaret Laurence and Adele Wiseman* (319). Margaret Laurence writes: "The main character, coming into this last chapter for the first time, talks awfully like you, I regret to say. I mean, she does and she doesn't. She isn't you, I need hardly say—but any fool who knows both of us would never believe I didn't base the character on you. ADELE I'M SORRY!!! I NEVER MEANT TO!"

My quick summary of "peaks" in Adele's work doesn't give the extent of her range. I haven't mentioned her charming memoir, *Old Markets, New Worlds*, her short stories (apart from "Goon of the Moon and the Expendables"), her unpublished children's play, *Someday Sam,* her published children's books, her unpublished letters, and other writing.

While I don't cite Kenneth Sherman's essay, "*Crackpot*: A Lurianic Myth" (published in *Waves* 3.1 (Autumn 1974): 4-11) my understanding of the themes of fragments, broken pots and Tikkun Olam is drawn from it.

Poems

I have included dates of the poems where possible.

I have selected the poems in this book both from the three hundred thirty-two that Adele considered finished and from the three earlier boxes of poetry. In many cases, Adele folded several drafts of poems inside the final version.

In a few cases, I have chosen a "draft" version rather than the final version.

The poems here are as Adele wrote them. I have noted minor textual problems (illegible revisions, for instance) as they appear.

Epigraphs to "In Our Play"

Loved one—these lines are the start of a longer poem about breath, dated July 23, 1982.

Anyone who has waited for a phone call, email, message or text from a Loved One will know the truth of this poem. I don't recommend holding your breath.

We should have been lovers: Idea note dated December 11, 1983, never worked into a typed poem.

"In Our Play"

"Rhymed Primal": Original title: "Rhymed Primal Haiku." In the manuscript "Haiku" is boxed and crossed out. Adele wasn't satisfied with "innocent" later in the poem, but she never corrected it.

"Send No Regrets": Last line originally read "I," amended to "I'll."

"It's winter now": "the strengthening" is crossed out, but there's no idea of what might have replaced it. This might be a reason why it was not included in Adele's final choice poems.

"Mysteries of Flight"

The order of the three "Summer Sunset" poems and "standards" is Adele's. They are grouped together in her "Mysteries of Flight" folder. In the next to last line of the third "Summer Sunset," Adele changed "is" to "see."

"The Dowager Empress Suite"

"Death of an Empress": line 10 — "the old witch": alternate reading in pencil: "tries (? illegible) to undermine the world we want to know."

Last line of first stanza: "And" underlined. "When" is a suggested substitute.

"But they never got the Empress": alternate version in pencil: "Did they ever get the Empress?" After the next two lines ("They got something but/ she wasn't what they thought" the alternate version suggests "Everyone wanted to get at her first…" which is seven lines down in the typescript.

"that foamed out of their mouths": "from" is cancelled and replaced by "out of."

Acknowledgements

I wish to thank Arlene Lampert, Adele's dear friend, for an earlier, much longer, selection of Adele's poems. I have built on her work and taken her choices into account as I compiled this book. I have also returned to the interview Arlene gave in *We Who Can Fly: Poems, Essays and Memories in Honour of Adele Wiseman* for valuable insights into Adele's poetry, her life, and her work.

Anyone who works on Adele Wiseman must be indebted to Ruth Panofsky for her superb scholarship and extensive bibliographical research, for her several pioneering projects on Adele. I follow in your footsteps, Ruth. Thank you!

Mary Lou Dickinson has been my companion in friendship for Adele since we met at Banff in 1992. I thank her for her companionship and for her encouraging response to the poems at a time when they were unheralded copies of unread pages in the York University Archives.

I am especially grateful to Tamara Stone for giving me permission to edit her mother's poetry and for the beautiful cover image. Thanks, Tamara, also, for your words about your mother's writing and poetry over the years. They have deepened my understanding of her work.

Great gratitude to David Laurence for allowing us to use his photograph of Adele, the best I have ever seen, as the author photo.

Special thanks to Luciana Ricciutelli, editor and publisher at Inanna, for her interest in the poems from the moment I mentioned them, through the incarnations of the manuscript, for her belief in and support of Adele's work.

Much gratitude to the archivists in the Clara Thomas Collection in the Scott Library at York University for their help—especially in locating "The Dowager Empress" at the back of one of the archival boxes in the Adele Wiseman Fonds.

And I am grateful to you, the reader, for letting Adele live again through your mind, eye, and breath.

Appendix: Original Contents of Wiseman's Files

Original contents of "In Our Play: Short verse by Adele Wiseman."
All capitalization is Adele Wiseman's.

1	The silent telephone
2	Experience, it seems
3	This strange invasion
4	Dangerous waters
5	I watched your eyes
6	Touching you, once
7	IN OUR PLAY
8	Sun through the window of the train
9	Just that pulse
10	RHYMED PRIMAL
11	SENRYU
12	How to make a fire
13	A good part of the art
14	We register degree of hurt
15	You enter
16	Some seek to become symbols
17	Winter passed without you
18	Permeable lover
19	A fertile underground
20	HAIKU
21	How many lovers driven driven
22	It's winter now

Original contents of "Mysteries of Flight: More short verse by Adele Wiseman"

Credits

"History Lesson" first appeared in *The Feminist Press: A Birthday Book* (New York: Feminist, 1988) p. 56.

"Ascent," "Roofers," and "Spaces" first appeared in *Poetry by Canadian Women*, ed. Rosemary Sullivan (Toronto: Oxford University Press, 1989) pp. 130-132.

"Ascent" was reprinted in *Poetry Alive: Perspectives,* ed. Don Saliani (Toronto: Copp Clark, Pitman, 1991) p. 88.

"Ascent," Roofers," and "Spaces" were reprinted in *Room of One's Own: A Space for Women's Writing* 16.3 (Sept. 1993), ed. Ruth Panofsky, pp. 86-89.

"Never Put A Poem Off," "Currents," and "The Gifted Itch-Scratcher" were published in *Juniper: An Online Poetry Journal,* 3.1 (June, 2019). Many thanks to founding editor Lisa Young.

Four of Adele's poems, not included in this selection, appear in Lenore Langs' "Adele as Poet and Inspirer of Poetry," *We Who Can Fly: Poems, Essays and Memories In Honour of Adele Wiseman* (Dunvegan, ON: Cormorant, 1997) pp. 113-123. The poems are on pages 120-123. Three of these poems, "Untitled: In the beginning always innocence," "Sound Wisdom Seen," and "Untitled: Someday when science has turned" were included in the three Annual Grand Wayzgoose publications (University of Windsor, 1990, 1991 and 1992). A fourth poem, "Tree House Song I," is also included in Lenore Langs' essay.

Works Cited

Works by Adele Wiseman:

Crackpot, Toronto: McClelland & Stewart, 1974.

"Goon of the Moon and the Expendables." *The Malahat Review* 98, (March 1992): 5-44. Reprinted in *We Who Can Fly: Poems, Essays and Memories in Honour of Adele Wiseman,* ed. Elizabeth Greene, (Dunvegan, ON: Cormorant, 1997) pp. 207-251.

Memoirs of a Book-Molesting Childhood and Other Essays. Toronto: Oxford University Press, 1987.

Old Markets, New World. Toronto: MacMillan 1964.

Old Woman at Play. Toronto: Clarke Irwin, 1978.

Poems including "The Dowager Empress Suite." Adele Wiseman Fonds FO447, Clara Thomas Archives, Scott Library, York University, 1981-92.

Testimonial Dinner. Toronto: Prototype Press, 1978. Printed Privately for the author.

The Lovebound: A Tragi-Comedy. c.1960. Adele Wiseman Fonds FO447. Clara Thomas Archives, Scott Library, York University.

The Sacrifice. New York: Viking; Toronto: Macmillan; London: Gollancz. 1956.

Interviews, Biography and Criticism:

Greene, Elizabeth, ed. *We Who Can Fly: Poems, Essays and Memories in Honour of Adele Wiseman.* Dunvegan, ON: Cormorant, 1997. Includes interviews with Arlene Lampert (pp. 55-61), Steven Heighton and Mary Cameron (pp. 80-90), as well as essays by Kenneth Sherman and Lenore Langs.

Langs, Lenore. "Adele As Poet and Inspirer of Poetry." *We Who Can Fly: Poems, Essays and Memories In Honour of Adele Wiseman*. Ed. Elizabeth Greene. Dunvegan, ON: Cormorant, 1997. 113-123.

Lennox, John and Ruth Panofsky, editors. *Selected Letters of Margaret Laurence and Adele Wiseman*. Toronto: University of Toronto Press, 1997.

Meyer, Bruce and Brian O'Riordan. "The Permissible and the Possible: An Interview With Adele Wiseman," *Lives and Works: Interviews by Bruce Meyer and Brian O'Riordan*. Windsor, ON: Black Moss Press, 1992. Reprinted in *Adele Wiseman: Essays on Her Works*, ed. Ruth Panofsky, Toronto: Guernica, 2001. 144-163.

Panofsky, Ruth, ed. *Room of One's Own* 16.3 (September 1993). Adele Wiseman Special Issue.

Panofsky, Ruth, ed. *Adele Wiseman: Essays on Her Works*. Writers Series 7. Toronto: Guernica, 2001.

Panofsky, Ruth. *The Force of Vocation: The Literary Career of Adele Wiseman*. Winnipeg: University of Manitoba Press, 2006.

Sherman, Kenneth. "*Crackpot*: A Lurianic Myth." Waves 3.1 (Autumn, 1974): 4-11. Reprinted in *e Who Can Fly: Poems, Essays and Memories in Honour of Adele Wiseman*. Dunvegan, ON: Cormorant, 1997. 167-73.

Sullivan, Rosemary. *Poetry by Canadian Women*. Toronto: Oxford University Press, 1984.

Adele Wiseman. Photo: David Laurence

Adele Wiseman (1928-1992) won the Governor General's Award in 1956 for her first novel, *The Sacrifice*. Her subsequent books included *Old Markets, New World*; *Crackpot*, winner of the Canadian Booksellers Association Award; *Old Woman at Play*; and *Memoirs of a Book-Molesting Childhood and Other Essays*. Her poetry, mostly unpublished before now, is the major work of her last ten years.

Photo: Alan Clark

Elizabeth Greene edited and contributed to *We Who Can Fly: Poems, Essays and Memories in Honour of Adele Wiseman*, winner of the 1998 Betty and Morris Aaron Prize for Best Scholarship on a Canadian Subject (Jewish Book Award). She has published three collections of poetry: *The Iron Shoes* (2007), *Moving* (2010), and *Understories* (2014) and a novel, *A Season Among Psychics* (2018). She lives in Kingston, Ontario.